Grants Thesaurus

Table of Contents

The Oryx Press
1986

The rare Arabian Oryx is believed to have inspired the myth of the unicorn. This desert antelope became virtually extinct in the early 1960s. At that time several groups of international conservationists arranged to have 9 animals sent to the Phoenix Zoo to be the nucleus of a captive breeding herd. Today the Oryx population is over 400 and herds have been returned to reserves in Israel, Jordan, and Oman.

2214 North Central at Encanto
Phoenix, Arizona 85004-1483

Printed and Bound in the United States of America

Published simultaneously in Canada

Library of Congress Card No. 86-60562
ISBN 0-89774-335-0
ISSN 0888-0581

Introduction

For over a decade the GRANTS database and its print complements, *Directory of Research Grants, Directory of Biomedical and Health Care Grants, Directory of Grants in the Humanities,* and *Directory of Grants in the Physical Sciences* have provided the sponsored-research community with current and accurate information regarding funding for programs, projects, scholarships, fellowships, conferences, and internships. Today with funding sources declining and funding amounts diminishing, the competition for funding is fiercer than ever. To meet the increased information needs of research professionals, the GRANTS database, researched and edited by members of the editorial staff of The Oryx Press, has increased significantly and now offers factual and concise descriptions of more than 5,000 funding programs.

IMPROVED SUBJECT ACCESS

A significant change has recently been made to the database, however, and that is the addition of subject terms to each grant program. Their presence on the database has made it possible for users of the GRANTS print products to consult a detailed, easy-to-use Subject Index to locate funding programs offered in their specific area(s) of interests. Now, online users may enjoy the same detailed access to subject terms listed in each funding program by consulting the *Grants Thesaurus.*

USING THE THESAURUS

Following are general guidelines that will make your search of the GRANTS database more successful. First, check under the specific topic of interest rather than a more general term. For instance, if you are interested in chemical engineering, look under Chemical Engineering rather than Engineering. Items indexed under Engineering indicate funding in broad areas of engineering only. There is no indication that the funding source will (or will not) fund grants in chemical engineering. However, if you don't locate the specific topic you are looking for, check a more general term. For example, grants concerning ballet are indexed under Dance.

Many grant programs provide funds for research- or performance-related scholarships, fellowships, faculty fellowships, dissertation support, internships, conferences, or undergraduate education. When grant funds are not limited by subject area, these grants are indexed under: Conferences, Meetings, Seminars; Dissertations; Faculty Fellowships; Internship Programs; Scholarships and Fellowships; or Undergraduate Education. If grant funds are designated for specific disciplines, you'll find the items under the specific subject: Art (Scholarships and Fellowships); Chemical Engineering (Faculty Fellowships); Photography (Internships); Cancer (Conferences) or Accounting (Undergraduate Education).

Grants concerning study of a particular country are listed under the name of the country. Grants concerning the history, literature, art, and language of a country are listed under the name of the country also: Greek History, Greek Literature, Greek Art, and Greek Language.

Grants for research and study in other countries are listed under Study Abroad or Travel and Exchange Programs if there is no specific country indicated in the grant program. Grants for study or travel to specific countries are listed under the name of the country or the continent: Japan (Travel and Study Grants); Africa (Travel and Study Grants).

The editors would like to thank Linda Webster for the construction of this thesaurus and the assignment of the index terms to each program listed. And to Anne Rhodes for her diligent research and editorial work.

A

Abortion (see also Family Planning; Reproductive Biology)
Academic Libraries
Academic Libraries (Internship Programs)
Accessibility (For Disabled)
Accident Prevention (see also Fire Safety; Highway Safety; Occupational Health and Safety; Safety; Water Safety)
Accounting
Accounting (Dissertation Support)
Accounting (Scholarships and Fellowships)
Accounting (Undergraduate Education)
Accounting Education
Acoustics
Acting *See* Theater Arts
Actuarial Science *See* Insurance
Addictive Behavior *See* Alcoholism; Community Outreach Programs; Drug Abuse; Mental Health
Administration (see also Art Administration; Educational Administration; Health Care Administration; Hotel/Restaurant Administration; Library Administration; Management Development; Public Administration; Social Services Administration)
Adolescent Pregnancy
Adolescent Psychology
Adolescents (see also Delinquency; Disabled Youth; Disadvantaged Youth; Dropouts; Runaway Youth; Young Adult Literature; Youth Employment; Youth Programs and Services
Adoption (see also Youth Programs and Services)
Adult Education (see also Continuing Education; Inservice Teacher Education; Job Training; Literacy Education; Medical Continuing Education)
Advertising (see also Public Relations)
Aeronomy (see also Atmospheric Science)
Aerospace Education
Aerospace Medicine
Aerospace Science
Aerospace Science (Dissertation Support)
Aerospace Science (Faculty Fellowships)
Aerospace Science (Scholarships and Fellowships)
Aerospace Technology (see also Astronomy; Atmospheric Science; Aviation Technology; Lunar Research)
Aerospace Technology (Dissertation Support)
Aerospace Technology (Faculty Fellowships)

Aerospace Technology (Scholarships and Fellowships)
Affirmative Action (see also Equal Opportunities)
Africa (see also names of specific countries)
Africa (Scholarships and Fellowships)
Africa (Travel and Study Grants)
African Art
African History
African Languages
Afro-Americans *See* Blacks
Age Discrimination
Aging *See* Geriatrics; Gerontology; Retirement; Senior Citizens Programs and Services
Agribusiness
Agricultural Chemicals (see also Pesticides)
Agricultural Education
Agricultural Extension
Agriculture (see also Agronomy; Animal Husbandry; Aquaculture; Entomology; Farm Management; Fertilizers; Floriculture; Forestry; Genetics; Plant Pathology; Veterinary Science)
Agriculture (Scholarships and Fellowships)
Agriculture (Undergraduate Education)
Agronomy (see also Plant Pathology)
AIDS (see also Sexually Transmitted Diseases)
Air Conditioning (see also Cooling Systems)
Air Pollution
Air Transportation (see also Aerospace Technology; Aviation Technology)
Alabama
Alaska
Alaskan Natives
Albania
Albania (Travel and Study Grants)
Alcoholism
Algebra (see also Mathematics)
Allergic Diseases and Disorders (see also Immunology)
Allied Health Sciences
Allied Health Sciences (Scholarships and Fellowships)
Alternative Energy Sources *See* Energy; Fuels; Nuclear Energy; Solar Energy; Wind Energy
Alzheimer's Disease *See* Geriatrics
American History *See* United States History
American Indian Education
American Indian Employment
American Indian Studies
American Indian Studies (Scholarships and Fellowships)
American Indians
American Studies

American Studies (Dissertation Support)
American Studies (Scholarships and Fellowships)
Anemia *See* Blood Diseases and Disorders
Anesthesiology
Animal Husbandry (see also Veterinary Science)
Animal Resources *See* Research Resources
Animals *See* Animal Husbandry; Pets; Veterinary Medicine; Veterinary Science; Zoology; Zoos
Anorexia Nervosa *See* Behavioral and Mental Disorders
Antarctica
Anthropology (see also Archaeology; Ethnology)
Anthropology (Conferences)
Anthropology (Dissertation Support)
Anthropology (Scholarships and Fellowships)
Antibiotics *See* Pharmacology
Anticonvulsants *See* Epilepsy; Pharmacology
Appalachia
Apprenticeships *See* Art (Internship Programs); Performing Arts (Internship Programs)
Aptitude Testing
Aquaculture
Archaeology (see also Anthropology)
Archaeology (Dissertation Support)
Archaeology (Faculty Fellowships)
Archaeology (Scholarships and Fellowships)
Architectural Education
Architectural History
Architectural History (Dissertation Support)
Architectural History (Scholarships and Fellowships)
Architecture (see also Building Grants; Landscape Architecture; Preservation Programs)
Architecture (Dissertation Support)
Architecture (Scholarships and Fellowships)
Architecture (Undergraduate Education)
Archives (see also Libraries; Museums)
Arctic Studies
Area Studies *See* American Studies; Canadian Studies; Developing Countries; Foreign Languages; International Affairs; International Studies; and names of specific countries
Argentina
Argentina (Travel and Study Grants)
Arizona
Arkansas
Armed Forces *See* Military Personnel
Arms Control *See* Disarmament

Art (see also Computer Applications (Arts); Design; Film Production; Fine Arts; Folk Art; Graphic Arts; Handicrafts; Humanities; Interior Design; Media Arts; Music; Painting; Photography; Sculpture; Theater Arts; Touring Arts Programs; Video Production; Visual Arts; and names of specific countries, such as Italian Art)
Art (Conferences)
Art (Dissertation Support)
Art (Internship Programs)
Art (Scholarships and Fellowships)
Art (Undergraduate Education)
Art, Experimental
Art Administration
Art Administration (Internship Programs)
Art Criticism
Art Education
Art Galleries *See* Museums
Art History
Art History (Dissertation Support)
Art History (Faculty Fellowships)
Art History (Internship Programs)
Art History (Scholarships and Fellowships)
Arthritis (see also Rheumatology)
Artificial Intelligence
Artificial Organs (see also Organ Transplants)
Artist-Run Centers
Artists' Colonies
Artists in Residence
Asia (see also names of specific countries)
Asia (Scholarships and Fellowships)
Asia (Travel and Study Grants)
Asian Americans (see also Minority Groups)
Asian Art
Asian History
Asian Languages
Associations *See* Community Organizations; International Organizations; Organizations (Groups); Professional Associations
Asthma *See* Respiratory Diseases and Disorders
Astronomy (see also Aerospace Science; Aerospace Technology; Lunar Research; Solar System)
Astronomy (Faculty Fellowships)
Astronomy (Scholarships and Fellowships)
Astronomy Education
Astrophysics
Astrophysics (Dissertation Support)
Astrophysics (Scholarships and Fellowships)
Athletics (see also Physical Education)

Atmospheric Science (see also Aeronomy; Climatology; Meteorology)
Atmospheric Science (Dissertation Support)
Atmospheric Science (Faculty Fellowships)
Atmospheric Science Education
Atomic Energy *See* Nuclear Energy
Atomic Physics *See* Physics
Audio Production
Audio Production (Conferences)
Audiology (see also Otorhinolaryngology; Speech and Hearing Disorders)
Audiovisual Materials *See* Documentaries; Films; Nonprint Media; Videotape Recordings
Audiovisual Production *See* Audio Production; Film Production; Television and Radio; Video Production
Australia
Australia (Travel and Study Grants)
Australian Literature
Austria
Austria (Travel and Study Grants)
Austrian Art
Austrian History
Austrian Literature
Autism *See* Behavioral and Mental Disorders
Automated Clinical Analysis *See* Medical Technology
Automation *See* Office Automation; Technology; and headings beginning with Computer
Aviation History
Aviation Technology (see also Aeropsace Technology; Flight Training)

B

Burma
Burma (Travel and Study Grants)
Burns and Trauma
Business (see also Accounting; Banking and Finance; Economics; Employment; Government Business Relationship; Industry; International Trade; Labor Relations; Marketing; Minority Businesses; Retailing; Small Businesses; University Business Relations; Women in Business)
Business Administration (see also Management Development)
Business Administration (Conferences)
Business Administration (Dissertation Support)
Business Administration (Faculty Fellowships)
Business Administration (Internship Programs)
Business Administration (Scholarships and Fellowships)
Business Administration (Student Loans)
Business Administration (Undergraduate Education)
Business Administration Education
Business Education (see also Office Occupations Education)
Business History
Business, International (see also International Trade)
Business Responsibility
Byzantine History

C

Computer Applications (Mathematical)
Computer Applications (Medical) (see also Behavioral Medicine; Medical Informatics; Medical Technology)
Computer Applications (Musical)
Computer Applications (Physical Sciences)
Computer Applications (Science)
Computer Assisted Construction
Computer Assisted Instruction (see also Educational Technology)
Computer Assisted Manufacturing
Computer Engineering
Computer Graphics
Computer Languages
Computer Literacy
Computer Networks
Computer Programming
Computer Science (see also Information Science)
Computer Science (Conferences)
Computer Science (Faculty Fellowships)
Computer Science (Internship Programs)
Computer Science (Scholarships and Fellowships)
Computer Science (Undergraduate Education)
Computer Science Education
Computer Simulation
Computer Software
Conferences, Meetings, Seminars (see also Continuing Education; Continuing Medical Education; Inservice Teacher Education; and specific topics of meetings, such as Humanities (Conferences))
Conflict Resolution
Congenital Defects *See* Birth/Congenital Defects
Congregationalism
Connecticut
Conservation (see also Air Pollution; Ecology; Energy Conservation; Environmental Programs; Forestry; Natural Resources; Pollution; Water Pollution; Wildlife Management)
Conservation (Scholarships and Fellowships)
Conservation of Buildings and Materials *See* Preservation Programs
Construction Grants *See* Building Grants
Construction Industry (see also Computer Assisted Construction)
Consultants
Consumer Behavior
Consumer Education
Continuing Education (see also Adult Education; Inservice Teacher Education; Management Development)
Continuing Medical Education
Contraceptives *See* Family Planning; Reproductive Biology
Cooling Systems (see also Air Conditioning)
Cooperative Education

Corporate Responsibility *See* Business Responsibility
Correctional Institutions
Correctional Rehabilitation
Correctional Rehabilitation (Conferences)
Cosmetic Science
Cost Effectiveness
Costa Rica
Countries *See* names of specific countries
Courts *See* Civil Justice; Criminal Justice; Law
Crafts *See* Folk Art; Handicrafts
Craniofacial Anomalies (see also Dentistry; Orthodontics; Plastic Surgery)
Creative Arts *See* Art; Dance; Film Production; Fine Arts; Music; Photography; Theater Arts; Video Production
Creative Writing *See* Children's Literature; Fiction; Literature; Poetry; Short Stories; Writing
Crime (see also Correctional Institutions; Correctional Rehabilitation; Delinquency; Law Enforcement)
Crime (Dissertation Support)
Crime Prevention
Criminal Justice
Criminal Justice (Dissertation Support)
Criticism *See* Art Criticism; Dramatic Criticism; Literary Criticism
Cubans
Culinary Arts (see also Food Service Industry)
Cultural Programs (see also Art; Artists in Residence; Dance; Fine Arts; Humanities; Libraries; Museums; Music; Performing Arts Centers; Theater Arts; Touring Arts Programs; Writers in Residence)
Curriculum Development
Cyprus (Travel and Study Grants)
Cystic Fibrosis
Cytology (see also Cellular and Molecular Biology)
Czechoslovakia
Czechoslovakia (Travel and Study Grants)

D

Developmental Biology (see also Genetics)
Diabetes Mellitus
Diagnostic Imaging *See* Medical Technology
Dialysis (see also Kidney Diseases and Disorders)
Diet *See* Nutrition
Digestive Diseases and Disorders (see also Gastroenterology)
Disabilities (see also Behavioral and Mental Disorders; Employment of Disabled; Learning Disorders; Mainstreaming; Mental Retardation; Special Education; Speech and Hearing Impairments; Visual Impairments; and names of other specific disorders and impairments)
Disabled Youth
Disadvantaged (see also Poverty; Poverty Programs)
Disadvantaged Schools (see also Minority Schools)
Disadvantaged Youth
Disarmament (see also Defense Technology; Nuclear Warfare; Peace)
Disarmament (Dissertation Support)
Disasters *See* Earthquakes; Emergency Medicine; Emergency Programs
Discrimination *See* Affirmative Action; Age Discrimination; Civil Rights; Equal Opportunities; Racial Discrimination; School Desegregation
Diseases and Disorders *See* specific names of diseases
Dissertation Support (see also names of disciplines, such as Psychology (Dissertation Support))
District of Columbia
Doctoral Dissertations *See* Dissertation Support; names of specific disciplines
Doctoral Fellowships *See* Scholarships and Fellowships; names of specific disciplines
Documentaries (see also Film Production; Television and Radio; Video Production)
Domestic Violence
Dominican Republic
Down's Syndrome *See* Mental Retardation
Drama *See* Playwriting; Theater Arts
Drawing *See* Visual Arts
Dropouts
Drug Abuse
Drugs *See* Drug Abuse; Pharmacology
Dutch Art *See* Netherlands (Art)

E

Education (Conferences)
Education (Faculty Fellowships)
Education (Internship Programs)
Education (Scholarships and Fellowships)
Education, International
Education, Professional *See* Continuing Medical Education; Dental Education; Inservice Teacher Education; Legal Education; Library Science Education; Management Development; Medical Education; Nursing Education; Teacher Education
Education Service Centers
Educational Administration
Educational Assistance *See* American Indian Education; Black Education; Dissertation Support; Mexican American Education; Minority Group Education; Scholarships and Fellowships; Student Financial Aid; Women's Education; and names of specific disciplines, such as History (Dissertation Support) and History (Scholarships and Fellowships)
Educational Innovation
Educational Technology (see also Computer Assisted Instruction)
Educational Testing
Egypt
Egypt (Travel and Study Grants)
El Salvador
Elderly *See* Geriatrics; Gerontology; Retirement; Senior Citizens Programs and Services
Electrical Engineering
Electrical Engineering (Faculty Fellowships)
Electrical Engineering (Internship Programs)
Electrical Engineering (Scholarships and Fellowships)
Electrical Engineering (Undergraduate Education)
Electricity
Electrochemistry
Electromagnetism
Electronics
Electronics (Faculty Fellowships)
Elementary Education (see also Intermediate Grades)
Embryology
Emergency Medicine
Emergency Programs
Emotional Disturbances (see also Behavioral and Mental Disorders; Mental Health; Schizophrenia)
Employment (see also American Indian Employment; Black Employment; Fringe Benefits; Government Employees; Job Training; Mexican American Employment; Minority Group Employment; Staff Development; Women's Employment; Youth Employment)
Employment (Conferences)

Employment of Disabled
Endocrine Diseases and Disorders (see also Diabetes Mellitus; Endocrinology)
Endocrinology (see also Endocrine Diseases and Disorders; Neuroendocrinology)
Endorphins *See* Neurophysiology
Energy (see also Coal; Electricity; Fuels; Nuclear Energy; Petroleum Industry; Solar Energy; Wind Energy)
Energy (Dissertation Support)
Energy (Faculty Fellowships)
Energy (Internship Programs)
Energy (Scholarships and Fellowships)
Energy (Undergraduate Education)
Energy Conservation
Energy Conservation (Dissertation Support)
Energy Conservation (Faculty Fellowships)
Energy Conservation (Internship Programs)
Energy Education
Engineering (see also Aerospace Technology; Biotechnology; Chemical Engineering; Civil Engineering; Computer Applications (Engineering); Computer Engineering; Electrical Engineering; Electronics; Environmental Engineering; Human Factors Engineering; Hydraulics; Industrial Engineering; Mechanical Engineering; Medical Technology; Metallurgical Engineering; Nuclear Engineering; Process Engineering; Solid-State Engineering; Structural Engineering; Systems Engineering)
Engineering (Conferences)
Engineering (Dissertation Support)
Engineering (Faculty Fellowships)
Engineering (Internship Programs)
Engineering (Scholarships and Fellowships)
Engineering (Student Loans)
Engineering (Undergraduate Education)
Engineering Education
Engineering History
Engineering History (Dissertation Support)
England *See* Great Britain
English (see also Editing; Linguistics; Literature; Translation)
English (Scholarships and Fellowships)
English (Second Language)
English (Undergraduate Education)
English Education
Entomology
Entomology (Scholarships and Fellowships)
Environmental Engineering
Environmental Health
Environmental Health (Scholarships and Fellowships)

Environmental Programs (see also Air Pollution; Conservation; Ecology; Energy Conservation; Forestry; Natural Resources; Pollution; Water Pollution; Wildlife Management)
Environmental Programs (Conferences)
Environmental Programs (Faculty Fellowships)
Environmental Programs (Internship Programs)
Environmental Programs (Scholarships and Fellowships)
Environmental Programs (Undergraduate Education)
Epidemiology
Epidemiology (Scholarships and Fellowships)
Epilepsy
Equal Opportunities (see also Affirmative Action; Civil Rights; Racial Discrimination; School Desegregation)
Equipment Grants (see also Instrumentation; Research Resources)
Eskimos *See* Alaskan Natives
Esperanto
Ethics
Ethics (Conferences)
Ethics (Dissertation Support)
Ethics, Medical *See* Medical Ethics
Ethnic Groups *See* Alaskan Natives; American Indians; Asian Americans; Blacks; Cubans; Hispanics; Italian Americans; Japanese Americans; Jewish Studies; Mexican Americans; Migrant Programs; Minority Groups; Polish Americans; Puerto Ricans
Ethnic Studies (see also American Indian Studies; Black Studies; Jewish Studies; Mexican American Studies; Minority Groups)
Ethnic Studies (Scholarships and Fellowships)
Ethnography
Ethnology
Ethnology (Dissertation Support)
Europe (see also names of specific countries)
Europe (Scholarships and Fellowships)
Europe (Travel and Study Grants)
Europe, Eastern
Europe, Eastern (Travel and Study Grants)
European History (see also names of countries and historical periods)
European Languages (see also names of specific languages)
Evaluation Methods (see also Program Evaluation)
Exchange Programs *See* Travel and Exchange Programs
Exercise (see also Physical Education; Physical Medicine and Rehabilitation; Sports Medicine)
Exercise Physiology
Exhibits *See* Museums; Touring Arts Programs
Eye Diseases and Disorders *See* Ophthalmology; Visual Impairments

F

Finnish Language
Finnish Literature
Fire Safety
Fisheries
Flight Training (see also Aviation Technology)
Floriculture (see also Horticulture)
Florida
Fluoride Research (see also Cariology; Dentistry)
Folk Art (see also Handicrafts)
Folk Art (Conferences)
Folk Art (Internship Programs)
Folk Music
Folklore
Food *See* Nutrition
Food Service Industry (see also Culinary Arts; /Restaurant Administration; Meal Programs)
Food Service Industry (Scholarships and Fellowships)
Food Service Industry (Undergraduate Education)
Food Technology
Foreign Language Instruction
Foreign Language Instruction (Dissertation Support)
Foreign Language Instruction (Faculty Fellowships)
Foreign Language Learning
Foreign Languages (see also Classical Studies; Translation; names of specific languages)
Foreign Languages (Dissertation Support)
Foreign Languages (Faculty Fellowships)
Foreign Languages (Internship Programs)
Foreign Languages (Scholarships and Fellowships)
Foreign Languages (Undergraduate Education)
Foreign Policy (see also International Affairs; International Studies)
Foreign Students
Forestry
Forestry (Undergraduate Education)
Foster Care
France
France (Scholarships and Fellowships)
France (Travel and Study Grants)
French Art
French History
French Language
French Literature
Fringe Benefits
Fuels (see also Coal; Energy; Natural Resources; Petroleum Industry)
Funeral Industry
Fungal Diseases *See* Bacterial and Fungal Diseases; Mycology
Futures (of Society)

G

Gerontology (see also Geriatrics; Nursing Homes; Senior Citizens Programs and Services)
Gerontology (Conferences)
Gerontology (Scholarships and Fellowships)
Ghana
Gifted
Glaciology
Glaucoma *See* Ophthalmology; Visual Impairments
Government *See* Federal Government; Local Government; Political Science; Public Administration; Public Affairs; State Government
Government Business Relationship
Government Employees (see also Military Personnel)
Graduate Study *See* names of specific disciplines
Graphic Arts
Graphic Arts (Internship Programs)
Graphic Arts (Scholarships and Fellowships)
Graphic Arts (Undergraduate Education)
Great Britain
Great Britain (Art)
Great Britain (History)
Great Britain (Literature)
Great Britain (Scholarships and Fellowships)
Great Britain (Travel and Study Grants)
Greece
Greece (Scholarships and Fellowships)
Greece (Travel and Study Grants)
Greek Art (see also Classical Studies)
Greek History (see also Classical Studies)
Greek History (Dissertation Support)
Greek Language (see also Classical Studies)
Greek Literature (see also Classical Studies)
Grenada
Grief *See* Death and Dying
Group Dynamics
Group Homes
Growth Diseases and Disorders *See* Neuromuscular Diseases and Disorders; Physiology
Guatemala
Guinea (Travel and Study Grants)
Gynecology *See* Obstetrics/Gynecology

H

Haiti
Handicapped *See* Behavioral and Mental Disorders; Disabilities; Learning Disorders; Mainstreaming; Mental Retardation; Special Education; Speech and Hearing Impairments; Visual Impairments; and names of other specific disorders and impairments
Handicrafts (see also Folk Art)
Hansen's Disease
Hawaii
Health *See* Medical Programs/Projects (General); Mental Health; Preventive Medicine; Public Health
Health and Safety Standards *See* Occupational Health and Safety
Health Care Administration
Health Care Administration (Faculty Fellowships)
Health Care Administration (Scholarships and Fellowships)
Health Care Administration (Student Loans)
Health Care Delivery (see also Community Outreach Programs; Emergency Medicine; Health Maintenance Organizations; Hospices; Hospitals; Nursing; Nursing Homes; Preventive Medicine; Public Health; Women's Health Programs)
Health Care Delivery (Dissertation Support)
Health Care Financing *See* Financial Support; Health Care Administration; Health Insurance
Health Education (see also Continuing Medical Education; Dental Education; Medical Education; Nursing Education)
Health Education (Scholarships and Fellowships)
Health Insurance (see also Health Maintenance Organizations)
Health Maintenance Organizations
Health Sciences *See* Allied Health Sciences; Biomedicine; Dentistry; Medical Programs/Projects (General); Nursing; Veterinary Science
Hearing Impairments *See* Speech and Hearing Disorders
Heating
Hematology (see also Blood Diseases and Disorders)
Hematology (Faculty Fellowships)
Hemophilia *See* Blood Diseases and Disorders
Hepatology (see also Liver Diseases and Disorders)
Hepatology (Undergraduate Education)
Heredity *See* Genctics
Herpes Simplex (see also Sexually Transmitted Diseases)
High Schools *See* Secondary Education

Higher Education (see also Community Colleges; Faculty Development; Faculty Fellowships; Undergraduate Education; University Business Relations; and names of specific disciplines, such as Engineering Education and Engineering (Undergraduate Education)
Highway Safety
Highway Transportation
Hispanics *See* Cubans; Mexican Americans; Puerto Ricans
Historic Preservation *See* Preservation Programs
History (see also Archives; Classical Studies; Documentaries; Local History; Oral History; Preservation Programs; United States History and names of specific disciplines, states, countries, continents and historical periods, such as Architectural History, French History, Military History, Renaissance, Texas History)
History (Conferences)
History (Dissertation Support)
History (Faculty Fellowships)
History (Scholarships and Fellowships)
History Education
Holland *See* Netherlands
Holography
Home Economics
Home Economics (Faculty Fellowships)
Home Economics (Scholarships and Fellowships)
Home Economics Education
Honduras
Hong Kong
Horticulture (see also Floriculture)
Horticulture (Scholarships and Fellowships)
Horticulture (Undergraduate Education)
Hospices (see also Death and Dying)
Hospitals
Hotel/Restaurant Administration
Housing
Human Factors Engineering
Human Rights *See* Civil Rights
Human Services *See* Health Care Delivery; Poverty Programs; Senior Citizens Programs and Services; Social Services; Youth Programs and Services
Humanities (see also Art; Fine Arts; Literature; Music; Philosophy; Religion; Theater Arts; Theology)
Humanities (Conferences)
Humanities (Dissertation Support)
Humanities (Faculty Fellowships)
Humanities (Scholarships and Fellowships)
Humanities (Undergraduate Education)
Humanities Education

Humanities Education (Faculty Fellowships)
Humor
Hungary
Hungary (Travel and Study Grants)
Hunger *See* Nutrition; Poverty Programs
Hydraulics
Hydrology (see also Water Resources)
Hydrology (Scholarships and Fellowships)
Hypertension (see also Cardiovascular Diseases and Disorders)

I

Institutional Care *See* Correctional Institutions; Deinstitutionalization; Group Homes; Hospitals; Nursing Homes
Institutional Libraries
Institutional Schools
Instruction (see also Computer Assisted Instruction; Curriculum Development; Education; Educational Technology; Foreign Language Instruction; and names of specific disciplines, such as Art Education)
Instructional Materials (see also Films; Videotape Recordings)
Instrumental Music *See* Chamber Music; Music; Musical Instruments; Orchestras; Organ Music; Piano Music; Violin Music
Instrumentation (see also Equipment Grants; Research Resources)
Insurance (see also Health Insurance)
Insurance (Dissertation Support)
Insurance (Faculty Fellowships)
Insurance Education (Scholarships and Fellowships)
Interdisciplinary Approach (see also interdisciplinary subjects such as, Ethnic Studies, Women's Studies)
Interior Design (see also Design)
Interior Design (Faculty Fellowships)
Interior Design (Scholarships and Fellowships)
Intermediate Grades
Internal Medicine (see also Biomedicine; and names of diseases and medical specialties)
Internal Medicine (Faculty Fellowships)
International Affairs (see also Foreign Policy; names of countries and continents)
International Affairs (Conferences)
International Affairs (Faculty Fellowships)
International Affairs (Internship Programs)
International Affairs (Scholarships and Fellowships)
International Organizations
International Students *See* Foreign Students
International Studies (see also Foreign Policy; names of specific countries and continents)
International Studies (Conferences)
International Studies (Dissertation Support)
International Studies (Faculty Fellowships)
International Studies (Internship Programs)
International Studies (Scholarships and Fellowships)
International Studies (Undergraduate Education)
International Trade (see also Business, International; Economics, International)
International Travel *See* Study Abroad; Travel and Exchange Programs; names of specific countries and continents, such as France (Travel and Study Grants)

Internship Programs (see also names of disciplines and work settings, such as Art (Internship Programs); Federal Government (Internship Programs)
Interpreters (see also Translation)
Iowa
Iraq (Travel and Study Grants)
Ireland
Ireland (Travel and Study Grants)
Islamic Culture
Israel
Israel (Scholarships and Fellowships)
Israel (Travel and Study Grants)
Italian Americans
Italian Art (see also Classical Studies)
Italian History (see also Classical Studies)
Italian Language (see also Classical Studies)
Italian Literature (see also Classical Studies)
Italy
Italy (Travel and Study Grants)

J, K

L

Labor Movement
Labor Relations (see also Employment)
Landscape Architecture
Landscape Architecture (Scholarships and Fellowships)
Language Arts *See* English Education
Language Disorders *See* Speech and Hearing Disorders
Languages *See* English; Esperanto; Foreign Languages; names of specific languages, such as French Language
Laos
Lasers
Latin America (see also South America; names of specific countries)
Latin America (Scholarships and Fellowships)
Latin America (Travel and Study Grants)
Latin American History
Latin American History (Dissertation Support)
Latin Language
Law (see also Civil Justice; Criminal Justice; Legal Education; Legal History)
Law (Dissertation Support)
Law, International
Law Enforcement (see also Correctional Institutions; Crime; Criminal Justice; Delinquency)
Law Libraries
Law Schools *See* Legal Education
Lead
Leadership
Learning Disorders (see also Memory and Cognitive Processes)
Legal Aid
Legal Education
Legal Education (Faculty Fellowships)
Legal Education (Internship Programs)
Legal Education (Scholarships and Fellowships)
Legal Education (Undergraduate Education)
Legal History
Leisure *See* Parks; Recreation
Leprosy *See* Hansen's Disease
Leukemia
Liberia (Travel and Study Grants)
Libraries (see also Academic Libraries; Archives; Computer Applications (Libraries); Film Libraries; Institutional Libraries; Law Libraries; Medical Libraries; Public Libraries; Reference Materials; School Libraries; Special Libraries; State Libraries)

Libraries (Internship Programs)
Library Administration
Library Networks
Library Science (see also Information Science)
Library Science (Dissertation Support)
Library Science (Faculty Fellowships)
Library Science (Scholarships and Fellowships)
Library Science Education
Life Sciences *See* Agriculture; Biology; Botany; Entomology; Genetics; Marines Sciences; Zoology
Linguistics
Literacy Education (see also Basic Skills)
Literary Criticism (see also Dramatic Criticism)
Literary Magazines
Literature (see also Children's Literature; English; Foreign Languages; Writing; Young Adult Literature; and names of specific countries, such as French Literature
Literature (Conferences)
Literature (Dissertation Support)
Literature (Faculty Fellowships)
Literature (Scholarships and Fellowships)
Liver Diseases and Disorders (see also Hepatology)
Loans *See* Student Financial Assistance
Local Government (see also State Government)
Local Government (Internship Programs)
Local History
Louisiana
Louisiana History
Low-Income Persons *See* Disadvantaged; Poverty; Poverty Programs
Lunar Research (see also Astronomy)
Lunch Programs *See* Meal Programs
Lung Diseases and Disorders *See* Pulmonary Diseases and Disorders
Lutheran Church

M

Mathematics (Undergraduate Education)
Mathematics Education
Mathematics History
Mathematics History (Dissertation Support)
Mauritania
Meal Programs (see also Nutrition)
Mechanical Engineering
Mechanical Engineering (Scholarships and Fellowships)
Mechanical Engineering (Undergraduate Education)
Mechanics (Physics)
Media *See* Audio Production; Documentaries; Film Production; Journalism; Mass Media; News Media; Nonprint Media; Television and Radio; Video Production
Media Arts (see also Documentaries; Film Production; Television and Radio; Video Production)
Medical Diagnostics/Imaging *See* Medical Technology
Medical Education (see also Allied Health Sciences; Biomedicine (Undergraduate Education); Continuing Medical Education; Dental Education; Health Education; Nursing Education; Pharmaceutical Education)
Medical Education (Faculty Fellowships)
Medical Education (Internship Programs)
Medical Education (Scholarships and Fellowships)
Medical Education (Student Loans)
Medical Ethics
Medical Informatics (see also Medical Libraries)
Medical Instrumentation *See* Medical Technology
Medical Libraries (see also Medical Informatics)
Medical Programs/Projects (General) (see also Biomedicine; Dentistry; Health Care Delivery; and names of specific diseases)
Medical Research *See* Biomedicine; names of specific diseases
Medical Technology (see also Biotechnology; Computer Applications (Medical); Microscopy; Nuclear Medicine)
Medical Technology (Scholarships and Fellowships)
Medicine *See* Biomedicine; Child/Maternal Health; Chiropractic; Health Care Delivery; Medical Programs/Projects (General); Osteopathic Medicine; Pediatrics; Preventive Medicine; Women's Health Programs; and names of other medical specializations and diseases
Medieval History (see also European History)
Mediterranean Countries (see also names of specific countries)
Mediterranean Countries (Scholarships and Fellowships)
Mediterranean Countries (Travel and Study Grants)
Meetings *See* Conferences, Meetings, Seminars; and specific disciplines, such as Humanities (Conferences)
Melanesia
Melanesia (Scholarships and Fellowships)

Memory and Cognitive Processes (see also Learning Disorders)
Mental Disorders *See* Behavioral and Mental Disorders
Mental Health (see also Adolescent Psychology; Behavioral and Mental Disorders; Child Psychology; Community Outreach Programs; Emotional Disturbances; Family Therapy; Music Therapy; Psychiatry; Psychology)
Mental Health (Internship Programs)
Mental Health (Scholarships and Fellowships)
Mental Retardation
Metabolic Diseases and Disorders (see also Diabetes Mellitus)
Metallurgical Engineering
Metallurgical Engineering (Undergraduate Education)
Metallurgy
Metallurgy (Faculty Fellowships)
Metallurgy (Internship Programs)
Metallurgy (Undergraduate Education)
Meteorology (see also Atmospheric Science)
Methodist Church
Mexican American Education
Mexican American Employment
Mexican American Studies
Mexican American Studies (Scholarships and Fellowships)
Mexican Americans
Mexico
Mexico (Scholarships and Fellowships)
Mexico (Travel and Study Grants)
Michigan
Microbiology
Microbiology (Scholarships and Fellowships)
Microbiology (Undergraduate Education)
Microcomputers (see also headings beginning with Computer)
Microscopy
Middle Ages *See* Medieval History
Middle East *See* Near and Middle East
Midwives
Migrant Education (see also Minority Group Education)
Migrant Programs (see also Mexican Americans; Minority Groups)
Military Affairs
Military History
Military History (Dissertation Support)
Military Personnel
Military Training
Mime (see also Theater Arts)
Mineralogy (see also Geology)
Mineralogy (Dissertation Support)
Mining
Minnesota

Minority Businesses (see also Small Businesses; Women in Business)
Minority Group Education (see also American Indian Education; Black Education; Mexican American Education)
Minority Group Employment (see also American Indian Employment; Black Employment; Mexican American Employment)
Minority Groups (see also Alaskan Natives; American Indians; Asian Americans; Blacks; Cubans; Ethnic Studies; Hispanics; Italian Americans; Japanese Americans; Jewish Studies; Mexican Americans; Migrant Programs; Polish Americans; Puerto Ricans)
Minority Schools (see also Disadvantaged Schools)
Missouri
Molecular Biology *See* Cellular and Molecular Biology
Molecular Physics *See* Physics
Mongolia (Travel and Study Grants)
Montana
Multidisciplinary Programs *See* Interdisciplinary Approach; and interdisciplinary subjects, such as Ethnic Studies; Women's Studies
Multiple Sclerosis
Municipal Government *See* Local Government
Muscular Dystrophy
Musculoskeletal Diseases and Disorders (see also Musculoskeletal System)
Musculoskeletal System (see also Musculoskeletal Diseases and Disorders)
Museums
Museums (Conferences)
Museums (Internship Programs)
Museums (Scholarships and Fellowships)
Music (see also Chamber Music; Computer Applications (Music); Dance; Jazz; Opera; Orchestras; Organ Music; Piano Music; Violin Music; Vocal Music)
Music (Conferences)
Music (Internship Programs)
Music (Scholarships and Fellowships)
Music, Experimental
Music Education
Music History
Music Recording
Music Therapy
Music Therapy (Scholarships and Fellowships)
Musical Composition
Musical Composition (Scholarships and Fellowships)
Musical Instruments
Musical Theater

Musicology
Muslim Culture *See* Islamic Culture
Mycology

N

Nigeria
Nigeria (Travel and Study Grants)
Nonprint Media (see also Audio Production; Film Production; Films; Media Arts; Television and Radio; Video Production; Videodisc Recordings; Videotape Recordings)
Nontraditional Learners
North America *See* Canada; United States
North Carolina
North Dakota
Norway
Norway (Travel and Study Grants)
Norwegian Language
Norwegian Literature
Novels *See* Fiction; Writing
Nuclear Energy (see also Defense Technology; Nuclear Engineering; Radiation)
Nuclear Engineering
Nuclear Engineering (Internship Programs)
Nuclear Engineering (Scholarships and Fellowships)
Nuclear Engineering (Undergraduate Education)
Nuclear Engineering Education
Nuclear Medicine
Nuclear Physics
Nuclear Science
Nuclear Science (Scholarships and Fellowships)
Nuclear Science (Undergraduate Education)
Nuclear Science Education
Nuclear Technology
Nuclear Warfare
Nuclear Waste
Numismatics
Nursing
Nursing (Faculty Fellowships)
Nursing (Internship Programs)
Nursing (Scholarships and Fellowships)
Nursing (Student Loans)
Nursing (Undergraduate Education)
Nursing Education
Nursing Homes
Nutrition (see also Meal Programs)
Nutrition (Scholarships and Fellowships)
Nutrition (Undergraduate Education)
Nutrition Education
Nutritional Diseases

O

Organizational Development
Organizations (Groups) (see also Community Organizations; International Organizations; Professional Associations)
Oriental Art *See* Chinese Art; Japanese Art
Orientals *See* Asian Americans
Ornithology (see also Biology; Zoology)
Orthodontics (see also Craniofacial Anomalies; Dentistry; Oral Diseases and Disorders)
Orthopedic Impairments (see also Orthopedics)
Orthopedics (see also Orthopedic Impairments)
Orthopedics (Conferences)
Osteopathic Medicine
Osteopathic Medicine (Internship Programs)
Osteopathic Medicine (Scholarships and Fellowships)
Osteopathic Medicine (Student Loans)
Osteopathic Medicine (Undergraduate Education)
Otorhinolaryngology (see also Audiology; Speech and Hearing Disorders)

P, Q

Personnel *See* Employment; Government Employees; Military Personnel; Paraprofessional Personnel
Personnel Development *See* Job Training; Staff Development
Personnel Management
Personnel Selection
Peru
Pesticides
Petroleum Industry
Petroleum Industry (Scholarships and Fellowships)
Petrology
Petrology (Dissertation Support)
Pets
Pharmaceutical Education
Pharmaceutical Education (Faculty Fellowships)
Pharmaceutical Education (Scholarships and Fellowships)
Pharmaceutical Education (Student Loans)
Pharmaceutical Education (Undergraduate Education)
Pharmaceuticals (see also Pharmacology)
Pharmacology (see also Chemotherapy; Pharmaceuticals)
Pharmacology (Conferences)
Pharmacology (Faculty Fellowships)
Pharmacology (Scholarships and Fellowships)
Pharmacy
Philippines
Philippines (Scholarships and Fellowships)
Philippines (Travel and Study Grants)
Philology *See* Linguistics; Literature
Philosophy
Philosophy (Dissertation Support)
Photogrammetry
Photography
Photography (Internship Programs)
Photography (Scholarships and Fellowships)
Physical Education (see also Athletics; Exercise)
Physical Education (Faculty Fellowships)
Physical Education (Scholarships and Fellowships)
Physical Medicine and Rehabilitation
Physical Medicine and Rehabilitation (Scholarships and Fellowships)
Physical Sciences (see also Astronomy; Chemistry; Computer Applications (Physical Sciences); Earth Sciences; Geology; Physics)
Physical Sciences (Conferences)
Physical Sciences (Dissertation Support)
Physical Sciences (Faculty Fellowships)
Physical Sciences (Internship Programs)
Physical Sciences (Scholarships and Fellowships)
Physical Sciences (Undergraduate Education)

Physical Sciences Education
Physical Sciences History
Physical Sciences History (Dissertation Support)
Physically Handicapped *See* Disabled Youth; Disabilities; Employment of Disabled; Speech and Hearing Disorders; Visual Impairments; and names of specific disorders and impairments
Physics (see also Acoustics; Astrophysics; Biophysics; Detonation Science; Electromagnetism; Geophysics; Mechanics (Physics); Nuclear Physics; Optics; Radiation; Solid-State Physics)
Physics (Dissertation Support)
Physics (Faculty Fellowships)
Physics (Internship Programs)
Physics (Scholarships and Fellowships)
Physics (Undergraduate Education)
Physics Education
Physiology (see also Neurophysiology)
Piano Music
Piano Music (Scholarships and Fellowships)
Pilot Training *See* Flight Training
Planets *See* Astronomy
Planning (see also Community Development; Policy; Public Policy; Urban Planning)
Planning (Internship Programs)
Planning (Scholarships and Fellowships)
Plant Pathology
Plastic Surgery
Playwriting (see also Theater Arts)
Podiatry
Podiatry (Faculty Fellowships)
Podiatry (Scholarships and Fellowships)
Podiatry (Student Loans)
Podiatry (Undergraduate Education)
Poetry
Poland
Poland (Scholarships and Fellowships)
Poland (Travel and Study Grants)
Police *See* Law Enforcement
Policy (see also Foreign Policy; Planning; Public Policy)
Polish Americans
Polish History
Polish Language
Polish Literature
Political Science (see also Disarmament; Federal Government; Foreign Policy; International Affairs; International Studies; Local Government; Public Affairs; State Government)
Political Science (Conferences)
Political Science (Dissertation Support)

Political Science (Faculty Fellowships)
Political Science (Internship Programs)
Political Science (Scholarships and Fellowships)
Political Science Education
Pollution (see also Air Pollution; Environmental Health; Environmental Programs; Industrial Waste; Nuclear Waste; Radiation; Radiation Effects; Solid Waste; Water Pollution)
Polynesia
Polynesia (Scholarships and Fellowships)
Poor *See* Disadvantaged; Poverty; Poverty Programs
Population Biology
Population Biology (Conferences)
Population Biology (Dissertation Support)
Population Control *See* Family Planning; Reproductive Biology
Population Studies *See* Demography
Portugal
Portugal (Travel and Study Grants)
Portuguese Language
Portuguese History
Portuguese Literature
Poverty (see also Disadvantaged)
Poverty Programs (see also Senior Citizens Programs and Services; Social Services; Youth Programs and Services)
Pregnancy *See* Adolescent Pregnancy; Obstetrics/Gynecology; Perinatal Disorders; Women's Health Programs
Presbyterian Church
Preschool Education *See* Early Childhood Education
Preservation Programs (see also Archives; Libraries; Microform; Museums)
Preservation Programs (Conferences)
Preventive Medicine (see also Health Education; Public Health)
Preventive Medicine (Internship Programs)
Primary Grades *See* Elementary Education
Prisons *See* Correctional Institutions
Private Schools (see also Minority Schools)
Probability (see also Statistics)
Probation *See* Correctional Rehabilitation
Process Engineering
Productivity
Professional Associations (see also International Organizations)
Professional Education *See* Continuing Medical Education; Dental Education; Inservice Teacher Education; Legal Education; Library Science Education; Management Development; Medical Education; Nursing Education; Social Work Education; Teacher Education)
Program Evaluation (see also Evaluation Methods)
Programming *See* Computer Programming

Programming Languages *See* Computer Languages
Prosthetics
Psoriasis *See* Dermatology
Psychiatry (see also Behavioral and Mental Disorders; Emotional Disturbances; Mental Health; Psychology; Schizophrenia)
Psychiatry (Internship Programs)
Psychiatry (Scholarships and Fellowships)
Psychology (see also Adolescent Psychology; Behavioral Medicine; Child Psychology; Community Outreach Programs; Death and Dying; Family Therapy; Memory and Cognitive Processes; Mental Health; Music Therapy; Social Psychology)
Psychology (Dissertation Support)
Psychology (Faculty Fellowships)
Psychology (Internship Programs)
Psychology (Scholarships and Fellowships)
Psychology (Student Loans)
Psychology Education
Public Administration (see also Federal Government; Local Government; State Government)
Public Administration (Conferences)
Public Administration (Internship Programs)
Public Administration (Scholarships and Fellowships)
Public Administration (Undergraduate Education)
Public Affairs (see also Citizen Participation; Federal Government; International Studies; Local Government; State Government; Urban Affairs)
Public Affairs (Conferences)
Public Affairs (Scholarships and Fellowships)
Public Health (see also Health Education; Preventive Medicine)
Public Health (Internship Programs)
Public Health (Scholarships and Fellowships)
Public Health (Student Loans)
Public Libraries
Public Policy (see also Foreign Policy; Public Affairs)
Public Policy (Dissertation Support)
Public Policy (Scholarships and Fellowships)
Public Relations (see also Advertising)
Public Schools *See* Disadvantaged Schools; Education; Elementary Education; Intermediate Grades; Junior High Schools; Kindergarten; Secondary Education
Public Television *See* Television and Radio
Public Welfare *See* Social Services
Publishing Industry (see also Literary Magazines)
Publishing Industry (Conferences)
Publishing Support
Puerto Ricans
Puerto Rico

R

S

Social Sciences (see also Anthropology; Geography; History; Political Science; Psychology; Social Psychology; Sociology)
Social Sciences (Conferences)
Social Sciences (Dissertation Support)
Social Sciences (Faculty Fellowships)
Social Sciences (Internship Programs)
Social Sciences (Scholarships and Fellowships)
Social Sciences (Undergraduate Education)
Social Sciences Education (see also History Education; Political Science Education; Psychology Education)
Social Services (see also Community Outreach Programs; Poverty Programs; Senior Citizens Programs and Services; Social Work; Volunteers; Youth Programs and Services)
Social Services Administration
Social Work
Social Work (Scholarships and Fellowships)
Social Work Education
Sociology
Sociology (Conferences)
Sociology (Dissertation Support)
Sociology (Scholarsips and Fellowships)
Software *See* Computer Programs
Soil Science
Solar Energy
Solar Energy (Faculty Fellowships)
Solar System (see also Astronomy)
Solid-State Chemistry
Solid-State Engineering
Solid-State Physics
Solid Waste
South America (see also Latin America; names of specific countries
South America (Scholarships and Fellowships)
South America (Travel and Study Grants)
South American History
South Carolina
South Dakota
Soviet Union *See* USSR
Space Sciences *See* Aerospace Science; Aerospace Technology; Astronomy; Atmospheric Science
Spain
Spain (Scholarships and Fellowships)
Spain (Travel and Study Grants)
Spanish History
Spanish Language
Special Education (see also Mainstreaming)
Special Education (Scholarships and Fellowships)
Special Libraries (see also Law Libraries; Medical Libraries)

Switzerland
Switzerland (Travel and Study Grants)
Symphony Orchestras *See* Orchestras
Systems Analysis
Systems Engineering
Systems Engineering (Scholarships and Fellowships)
Systems Theory

T

Theology (see also Religion)
Theology (Dissertation Support)
Theology (Faculty Fellowships)
Therapy *See* Adolescent Psychology; Child Psychology; Family Therapy; Mental Health; Music Therapy; Occupational Therapy; Rehabilitative Programs
Theology (Scholarships and Fellowships)
Third World Countries *See* Developing Countries; names of specific countries
Thoracic Surgery *See* Surgery
Throat Diseases *See* Otorhinolaryngology
Thyroid Diseases and Disorders
Tobacco
Tobago *See* Trinidad and Tobago
Touring Arts Programs
Tourism
Toxicology
Toxicology (Scholarships and Fellowships)
Trade *See* Business; Business, International; International Trade
Training *See* Computer Assisted Instruction; Flight Training; Job Training; Management Development; Military Training; Staff Development
Transfusion Medicine *See* Blood Diseases and Disorders; Hematology
Translation (see also Interpreters)
Transplants (Organ) *See* Organ Transplants
Transportation (see also Air Transportation; Highway Transportation)
Transportation (Scholarships and Fellowships)
Trauma *See* Burns and Trauma
Travel and Exchange Programs (see also Study Abroad; names of countries and continents, such as Sweden (Travel and Study Grants))
Trinidad and Tobago
Tropical Biology
Tropical Diseases and Disorders (see also Tropical Medicine)
Tropical Medicine (see also Tropical Diseases and Disorders)
Tuberculosis *See* Pulmonary Diseases and Disorders
Tumors *See* Cancer; Oncology
Turkey
Turkey (Travel and Study Grants)
Tutorial Programs (see also Compensatory Education)

U

V

W

X, Y, Z